©2019 D'Nieka Marie

All rights reserved.

ISBN: 978-0-9996621-1-3

Black Unity Publishing LLC, St. Louis, MO

www.doperelationships.com

Cover art created by Afi Ese

"You are Worthy: Conquering Your Insecurities From Within"

CHAPTER 1: How The Insecurities Began

CHAPTER 2: How Insecurity Makes Us Feel About Ourselves

CHAPTER 3: What We Attract From Being Insecure

CHAPTER 4: What We Become From Being Insecure

CHAPTER 5: The Realization Of What We've Become

CHAPTER 6: Overcoming Our Insecurities

Chapter 1: How The Insecurities Began

Many of our insecurities begin in childhood. Those are our most impressionable moments where we are so unsure of ourselves and are desperately trying to figure out our place in this big world. It is during those precious times where we first begin to see and take mental notes on the people and things around us. It's where we watch and study how people tend to view and treat us as individuals.

Everything starts from inside the home. Our parents are our biggest influencers and role-models. They are the first ones to show us and teach us about who and what we are, and how we should be treated. If our parents are loving, nurturing, and encouraging in their attempts to teach us and guide us, then we are more likely to have a confidence and a good self-esteem about ourselves. If our parents are more scolding, harsh, critical, and abusive in their attempts to teach and guide us, the higher our chances are of feeling uncertain, unsure, and insecure about who we are.

Many of us don't even realize the impact that our parents may have had on us as children that have a lasting effect on our self-esteem even now, as adults. We think that insecurities just sort of happen out of the blue, and are not a direct result of us not feeling worthy enough, good enough, or being rejected by the people that are supposed to love and care for us the most.

Take some time out to ask yourself a few questions. Were your parents nurturing and loving towards you? Did they teach you that you are valuable and important? Did they take the time out to correct you with love and support instead of saying things like "you're stupid", "you're dumb", or calling you foul names? Or did they do nothing at all?

Having an uninvolved parent or guardian impacts the way we view ourselves, and our confidence, just as much as a parent or guardian that is present. It can make us feel that *we are not even important enough* to be involved with, loved, and cared for, which adds to a lower self-esteem. This can begin to play a role on our emotions, tricking us into believing that we are no good, invisible, and worthless. As human beings, especially children, we need to know that we are valued, loved, powerful, important, and worthy. When we are not being taught this, or at least shown this, we begin to doubt ourselves and feel out of place. If we are not being shown that we are loved, valued, and cherished by our parents and other important members in our life, we will begin to look for validation in other things and people outside of those individuals, to feel good about ourselves. And more often than not, the things and people that we may begin to look for validation in are not of the healthiest nature (drugs, alcohol, poor company, etc).

Not only does the things that are done to us or taught to us directly as children have an influence on our self-esteem, but also our environment and the things that we see. What we witness (especially as children) has a direct impact on how we perceive ourselves, and what we deem to be acceptable and normal behavior. If we witness our mother being treated a certain way by our father, or we witness our father being treated a certain way by our mother, we begin to internalize these things and accept it as normal. For example, if a daughter sees that her mother is insecure based upon what she allows people (specifically men) to do to her or say to her, she too can grow up to adopt that same behavior and become insecure herself. If her mother tolerates being treated poorly, she can one day grow up and get into those same types of relationships or surround herself with those same types of people, and begin to accept poor treatment as well. The same goes for young men.

This is why it is very important for us to be properly groomed as children to know our self-worth and value. Parents, Guardians, and other important role-models, should be instilling into us, and *showing* us *by example* our importance, so that we can grow into adults that have a strong sense of self-worth and not settle for anything less than greatness. Unfortunately, we are not being taught our great value at an early age and it is forcing us to accept poor treatment and have low self-esteem as we grow and mature.

When we go out into the real world and have to deal with our peers, we may even find ourselves gravitating towards certain individuals or groups based upon how we feel about ourselves internally. If we have a low self-esteem, we may tend to lean more towards people that treat us *poorly* or talk down to us, because we feel that kind of treatment is what we deserve. On the flipside, if we have a healthy self-esteem, we may gravitate towards individuals that treat us with *respect* because we feel *that kind* of treatment is what we deserve. All of this is a result of how we view ourselves and what we were subconsciously taught by our elders, parents, and guardians of how we should allow others to treat us.

Being insecure has many deeply-rooted seeds that most of us don't even realize are planted. We think that it's just the way that it has always been so we just write it off as "not that important". But have you taken the time out to *really* try to figure out what is causing you to be insecure *in the first place?* Have you ever thought about *why* you tend to go after people that treat you poorly? Have you taken the time out to figure out *why you allow* certain things that cause you harm to come into your life and *you accept it as normal?* Most of us have not tried to get to the *root* of our insecurities, and that's why this vicious cycle of feeling insecure does not escape us.

Many of us probably never even thought about what I have just mentioned about our parents, guardians, and loved ones playing an important role in our self-esteem. That's because we hardly ever try to go back to the roots, and instead try to deal with what we are feeling on a surface level. How do I know?--- Because *I too* was once that surface-level person trying to fix deeply-rooted problems.

As a child, I suffered from low self-esteem and many insecurities. I didn't understand *why* until later on into my adulthood. My insecurities stemmed from growing up in a household where my mother was absent, and having a father that really didn't know how to raise a young girl into becoming a young woman. I was lucky in the sense that I had a father that nurtured me and told me constantly that I was precious, but it still wasn't enough.

My father really was a loving father and took good care of me growing up. However, not having a mother around to teach you certain things like how to properly groom yourself, how to handle and/or carry yourself as a young woman, or how to be comfortable in your own skin, was something that I lacked and desperately needed. I was a very well-mannered, smart, and nice young girl, but I needed my mother to show me how a woman was supposed to have *confidence.* I needed for a *woman* to *show* and teach me that I should feel good about myself regardless of how I looked, dressed, what I had or didn't have, and so forth.

When I went to school, I was constantly teased about my long, untamed, poofy hair, my big lips, my gapped-teeth, my dingy clothing, and my intelligence. I didn't have my mother around to reassure me that I was beautiful no matter how fluffy and unkept my hair was. I didn't have my mother around to encourage me to ignore people regarding my physical features, and to accept the fact that being smart was not "lame" or "geeky"; but instead was something to be proud about and embrace as a young woman.

As children, its essential to have that positive reinforcement at home to let you know that you should always feel good about yourself, and demand respect no matter what. Young boys mostly need that positive reinforcement from Men, and young girls mostly need that positive reinforcement from Women. And as a young woman, not having a female role-model to instill into me that confidence that I needed, made me feel less than, and accept that the mean things that were being done to me was okay.

My father eventually got with a decent young woman that was able to give me that positive reinforcement that I desperately needed from a woman. It felt good to have a motherly-figure around that could relate to me, and what I was going through. I needed to know that I didn't have to be the most beautiful girl in the class to feel confident. I needed to know that being and feeling insecure *was not o*kay, and that is was not acceptable for people to talk bad to me and treat me poorly.

How many of us have grown up in a household where we *didn't* have that positive reinforcement to step in when we were feeling low and unsure of ourselves? How many of us *didn't* have people that could help us to redirect our focus and put us back on the right track? How many of us just went through our childhood into adulthood feeling that being treated like garbage was acceptable because that's all we've ever known? *Plenty* of us. And this is the reason why we are feeling so miserable, drained, hopeless, and INSECURE, as adults.

CHAPTER 2: How Insecurity Makes Us Feel About Ourselves

There's a lot of us adults running around with a bunch of unsorted-through baggage from our childhood and/or past. Whether it was from not feeling loved by our parents, being betrayed by someone we trusted, being teased or made fun of in school, being abused, (mentally, physically, emotionally, sexually) or feeling ignored and unsure of ourselves; we all are running away from our problems and trying to cover it up with fake smiles and false senses of security.

Insecurity is a *beast.* We know that we can not afford to continue walking around feeling like we are not worthy due to our past and present traumas. We desperately want to face this beast head-on so that we can get what we deserve out of life. But how can we do that when we are constantly being plagued by this feeling of not being good enough?

Being insecure makes us feel *powerless*. It zaps us of our energy to fight our issues, and defeats us before we can even throw a punch. We feel that our *life is shitty* because *we are shitty people that deserve* a shitty life. Maybe we were told that we weren't good enough by people that were closest to us. Maybe we were discarded and left to fend for ourselves by people that we loved the most. Maybe we got our hearts broken over and over again to the point that we just know that there has to be something wrong with *us* instead of the people that are hurting us. Thus, we are left with the feelings of doubt, pain, hopelessness, and regret, always following us around.

Everyday is a challenge for those of us that suffer from feeling insecure. We find it hard to *trust* people, *love* people, or *let our guards down*, because deep down inside we just *know* that this person *too*, will disappoint us. Insecurity makes us feel that everybody has some sort of hidden agenda or ulterior motive, and only wants to come into our lives to use us and tear us down more. Even if this person means us well, we still don't feel that they are genuine because deep down inside, we feel that we are not good enough to even be genuine *to*.

Being insecure attacks us from the inside out. Our minds are always drifting over to the negative side because we feel negatively about *ourselves*. We feel that something is wrong with us, and that is the reason why we are so unlucky when it comes to finding genuine people that truly care about us and love us.

We want desperately to not feel this way, but its so embedded into us that we feel that it is something that is just apart of who we are. This makes us feel trapped and stuck in our ways.

    We know that being insecure is a problem that we need to rid ourselves of. We are tired of feeling low, weak, and insignificant. We do our best to eliminate certain feelings, but these negative feelings keep finding ways to resurface into our everyday lives, bringing us lower. Some days are better than others, but nonetheless, this empty feeling of not being worthy enough of anything of real substance and value, keeps rearing its ugly head, forcing us to be right back where we started the day before.

There may have even been times when genuine people *did* come into our lives making us feel that it was finally okay to let our guards down and give them a chance. This person may have done everything right to us and did amazing things that others have never done for us. *Yet still,* we somehow allowed our insecurities to ruin that friendship or relationship in one way or another. Maybe we began to accuse them of things unfairly. Maybe we made up things in our minds about them due to our own feelings of being inadequate until we believed it to be true. Maybe we were so critical of that person and/or ourselves, that we ended up turning that person off and ultimately pushing them away.

These kinds of things happen because feeling insecure can make those around us feel hopeless as well. If you are constantly being too hard on yourself about everything, always thinking the worst, and you don't allow them to try to help you out of your insecurities, they can begin to feel like their role in your life is a lost cause. Why? Because they can start to figure "what's the point of me trying to reassure this person that they are good enough and I have their best interests at heart, if its always going to be met with resistance anyway?"

Its important for those of us that are battling with insecurity to try to be mindful of how we are making people around us feel. We sometimes can get so caught up in our own thoughts, feelings, and emotions, that we are not paying attention to the thoughts, feelings, and emotions of the people around us. Most times, when we are struggling with feeling insecure, we subconsciously begin to push people away and wonder why most of our friendships and relationships are failing. This is because we are vibrating on low and negative frequencies and it is repelling people with good hearts and intentions away from us.

There are some of us that are so caught up in our negative thoughts and feelings that stem from being insecure, that we are not even aware that we are insecure in the first place. This is very dangerous. If you are not aware that you are an insecure person, then you wont even know that you are repelling good things and people away from you. You also wont be aware that you have a problem that needs to be addressed and fixed.

Some of us may go through life feeling that we are no good, and always having a chip on our shoulder. We feel that everybody is out to get us and that we are overall unlucky people. We are constantly feeling insignificant and we don't even know that its due to us being insecure. You may know of a person that is this way or you may have even been a person that was this way, yourself. I personally was this type of insecure person and it was very difficult for me. I'd always feel down, ugly, unsure of myself, and constantly feeling that everyone around me was judging me, and I didn't know why. I tried to pretend that I was confident, but then there'd always be a person or situation to remind me of why I shouldn't be.

As unaware insecure people, we blame ourselves for everything wrong in our lives. When people treat us poorly, we try to justify it by saying things like "well, it was my fault" or "I deserved it" or "I should have done ___ to not make them treat me that way." It's an ongoing battle of self-defeat and self-pity. We are not aware that we deserve to be treated with respect and common decency. Instead, everyone is justified in their poor behavior towards us. After a while, we even begin to treat ourselves badly by saying how dumb we are, how ugly we are, and how worthless we are for no particular reason. We think these terrible things are true because we are oblivious to the fact that we have deeply-rooted problems stemming from being insecure.

As I stated earlier, it took me a while to realize that I was suffering from insecurity. People (close family members) would try to tell me that I was being too hard on myself and try to reassure me that I was *not* this ugly, non-important girl that had no real value that I could bring to this world. I found it hard to believe because I couldn't see it in myself, and there were these people around me (classmates, so-called friends, boyfriends etc) that were telling me otherwise. I figured the people that were trying to tell me that I *was* of some sort of significance were only saying those things to be nice and cheer me up. Not because it was factual.

Its funny how feeling or being insecure can make us believe all of the things that are wrong and/or negative about ourselves, but have a difficult time accepting anything good or positive about ourselves. Even when we should be celebrating our victories and giving ourselves praise, insecurity finds a way to swoop in and steal our joy by reminding us of what we could have done better. We hardly ever see the light at the end of the tunnel because deep down we feel that the tunnel has no ending.

Insecurity makes us feel that we have no real alliances. People that try to help us out of our darkness are deemed as "not reliable sources" or "fake" because we don't know and understand how a person could ever feel that we are anything more than worthless. The people that we crave validation from the most are showing us daily that we are not these "great" or "spectacular" people, so any other opinion outside of that is just not true. The feelings that we have about ourselves are not positive because we have not learned to love and accept ourselves for who we are. We have not taken the time to self-reflect and see all of the great things about us. Instead, we choose to diminish all of our great attributes and qualities while blowing up and magnifying our weak attributes and qualities.

    This is truly unfair treatment and behavior but it is all that we know and are familiar with. We cling to the negatives because the negatives are what have been beaten into us so much so, that it is embedded into our minds. Insecurity has stripped away from us our logical and positive thoughts and replaced them with irrational, self-hating thoughts that make us feel that it is impossible to be anything other than the train wrecks that we are. This makes it almost impossible to attract the right kind of people into our lives that mean us well.

Chapter 3: What We Attract From Being Insecure

Having these internal battles with insecurity tends to attract abusive people to us. Why? Because when you are not feeling good about yourself, you give off the vibe or energy of someone that is weak, easily manipulated, and craving acceptance. People that are of an abusive nature sense those qualities about you and pursue you because they see you as an easy target.ABUSIVE people want desperately to have control over a person that has issues with self-confidence, because they too are deep down insecure, and want to finally feel that they are above and beyond someone.

Insecurity attracts insecurity. No one that has a good or positive self-esteem is going to want to be involved for too long, or *at all,* with a person that doesn't feel strongly about themselves in a positive light. Confident and secure people want other confident and secure people in their company, because they need positive energy around them to feed off of and keep their spirits high. If you are insecure, you will give off a draining and depressing energy that will naturally repel people of a positive self-esteem away from you.

However, this goes even further than just being insecure and repelling people of a good nature away from you. In most instances when you are insecure, you don't even *want* people that have a high self-esteem around you because they make you feel inadequate and intimidated. This makes us go after and/or accept the people that are of an abusive nature because they are what we are naturally used to. Abusive people are the equivalent to how we feel of our self-worth and value on the inside, which is why they are easily accepted into the company of those of us who are insecure. They treat us the way that we feel we deserve to be treated.

We subconsciously (or consciously) invite these horrible people into our lives and make them feel as though they have power over us. These people begin to take advantage of our weaknesses and use them against us so that they can control our every move, thought, feeling, and emotion. They know that by us being in this constant state of emptiness, that they can fill us up with whatever they want to make us feel like they are important factors in our lives.

If you are not careful, and you are not aware of your insecurity issues, these people can swoop in and manipulate you to the point where you feel hopeless without them. They will try to make you feel as though you are powerless and insignificant by using their charm or even by force. This is why it is important for us to recognize the signs that we are suffering from insecurity, so that we are cognizant of the kinds of people that we may attract to us.

Abusive people are not always aware that they are being abusive, just the same as not all insecure people are aware that they are suffering from low self-esteem or insecurity. Sometimes, people are so caught up in being a certain way that they are not aware that they are practicing negative or abusive behavior. An abusive person may be attracted to a person that seems weak, unsure of themselves, and have low self-esteem, but not necessarily know the reason behind *why* they go after people that display these kinds of characteristics. They are not always aware that the reason as to why they are going after people that they feel they can easily control and manipulate, is because they *themselves* don't feel that they are powerful, strong, significant, or important on their own.

    Abusive people need to feel that they have power over a person or situation, so that they can begin to feel a sense of value and importance. They then use insecurities as a way to manipulate and mold people so that they can use them to their benefit. A person that is *not* insecure and *has confidence,* challenges an abusive person, which makes them feel inadequate, and ultimately exposes them as the sad and insecure people that they truly are at their core. This is one of the main reasons why abusive people do not typically target people that are not insecure.

Both, insecure and abusive people, thrive off of each other. They both feed off of the voids that they are feeling, and use one another to try to fill these voids. Its very ironic and confusing to say the least. Both parties do not realize that they are using one another for validation purposes, and it is causing them to prolong, or continue on with an unhealthy relationship. Deep down, they both do not know and understand that they are just looking for acceptance from someone, and most of all, a purpose for being.

The insecure person feels that they have some kind of purpose by providing the abusive person with some degree of love, patience, and understanding of *why* they behave the way that they do. Although the person that is insecure feels that the poor treatment that they are receiving is well-deserved, they still are somewhat aware that this kind of treatment is unfair. Deep down, they know that the abusive person would *not* be able to get away with such treatment on anybody else; and they feel that they are somehow helping this abusive person by trying to be understanding and sticking around.

On the flipside, the abusive person feels that their purpose is to somehow guide this insecure person, and give them direction by controlling the way they think, feel, and view themselves. Both, the abusive person as well as the insecure person, are in denial of what they are *truly* doing to one another, and masking the true intent of why they are together. Deep down inside, they both don't want to be alone, and are avoiding trying to get to the root causes as to why they are the way that they are. Getting to the root causes as to why one would choose to treat people poorly and/or accept poor treatment, would require you to do a lot of self-reflecting and holding yourself accountable. Quite frankly, it is a lot easier to sweep everything under the rug, than to deal with all of the ugly truths about ourselves.

If you are insecure, you may invite people that hurt you into your life time after time, and wonder why all of your relationships are failing. You don't see where its all going wrong and are not aware that you are only changing out different people that have the same tendencies. You don't realize that you are allowing different people to come into your life and dictate you, stripping you of your power. Instead, you only see all of these failed relationships that end with you feeling as though you are not good enough.

Its important for us to realize that if we are constantly getting the same negative results, then there is something that *we* need to change about *ourselves and the company that we keep*. Unfortunately, many of us that are insecure, only swap out the individual, but go after a person that has the *same* negative qualities and characteristics as the last person. We even begin to try to make excuses for them by justifying their poor treatment of us, as well as their position in our lives. We try to look beyond their abusive nature and see the good in them, and may even start to view their abuse as love. Sadly, we don't realize how dangerous this is until it is too late, and this person has abused us mentally, spiritually, physically, and emotionally, beyond our threshold of pain.

By allowing people to come in and out of your life that really don't mean you well or have your best interest at heart, you are stripping yourself of your basic human rights to be respected and treated with common decency. Tolerating this kind of behavior repeatedly is subconsciously making you numb to being treated terribly. You will find yourself in more and more abusive relationships because you have now subconsciously or consciously, programmed yourself to feel or think that this sort of ill treatment is acceptable.

If you are insecure, you have to take it upon yourself to be extra careful about who and what you allow into your life. People can mean you well or they can mean you harm; but its all about having discernment and gauging whether or not people are genuine in their attempts to love you. Sad to say, when you are used to being treated poorly, you are more accustomed to making excuses for people and keeping them in your life when they shouldn't be. You begin to have a major problem with confusing false and unhealthy relationships, for genuine love and healthy relationships. This is why it is most important to take time to yourself outside of a relationship until you can work on your self-worth, self-love, and self-confidence. If you refuse to take time alone to figure out your problems, you will find yourself constantly in abusive and/or failed relationships that you seem to never truly have a chance at saving.

Now, some of us that are struggling with insecurities can luck up and actually attract and become involved with a person that helps us to break down our barriers and love ourselves. This is very rare because as I stated earlier, many of us that suffer with low self-esteem and insecurity can give people that genuinely love and care about us a hard time. This happens because we have trouble accepting the fact that we are worthy and good enough to be honored, loved, and respected in a whole-hearted way. But sometimes, the right person can come into our lives at the right time and help us to conquer these internal issues.

This sometimes can catch us off guard. At first, it may be difficult for us to actually accept that we are valuable enough to be genuinely loved and cared for by a person. But after a while of keeping our guards down, we may actually see that this person truly means us well by their *actions*. Even if we are being difficult in their attempts to help us gain confidence, trust, and acceptance, this person stays persistent and doesn't give up on us like many have done before in our past.

Though it is rare for insecure people to attract these kinds of individuals into their lives, there are always exceptions to the rule. Sometimes, a person that is genuine sees greatness in you that you don't always see in yourself, and wants to help show you how amazing you are. If you happen to attract this kind of individual, pay attention to what they are telling you and most of all what they are *showing you,* so that you are not being dismissive. They could actually be helping you to have a breakthrough into your self-discovery. Its ultimately up to you to take heed to the signs and act upon them so that you can maneuver through or around the good and bad people and relationships. But as I stated earlier, many of us that suffer from low self-esteem and have insecurity issues, often times attract abusive people and get into unhealthy relationships. This causes us to become unhealthy, self-sabotaging, and vengeful individuals.

Chapter 4: What We Become From Being Insecure

"Hurt people, hurt people." That's a sentiment that I always hear in regards to people treating individuals badly. Although this statement is oftentimes overly used, it is still a very accurate statement. This is essentially what happens to many of us that suffer with insecurity that keep being mistreated by people that we think that we love, and that we feel should love us, too.
We eventually become fed-up and go from "victim" to "abuser"; aka "hurt people hurting people".

    After a while, we become tired of being everyone's doormat. We grow tired of feeling ashamed and unimportant. We have had enough of thinking that people really care about us and they don't. That's when we reach a breaking-point of not ever wanting to feel powerless ever again in our lives. We call ourselves *"taking our power back"* by becoming the same types of callous people that we despise.

As I stated before, there are many insecure people that are abusive. Not all insecure people are these timid, unconfident, docile creatures that are completely oblivious to the fact that they are suffering. Some of us *know* that we are suffering and choose to turn our pain *outward* instead of holding it in. We begin to find refuge in our destruction of other people, thinking that by us being cruel, overly hostile, or angry, that we are protecting ourselves. We don't know that we are bringing about the very situations that we are trying to shield ourselves away from.

How many of us were so tired of being walked all over that we now have become the people that walk all over people? How many of us have been so mistreated that we now mistreat other people as a coping mechanism? How many of us feel that it is better to make someone else feel insecure about *themselves,* than for us to ever feel insecure about *ourselves* again? *Plenty of us.* And this is because we have become a term that I like to refer to as *"Bitterly-Insecure"* individuals.

Bitterly-Insecure people are people that are deeply hurting, and crying out for help by lashing out on people, and taking out their aggressions in destructive ways. This type of individual does not trust anybody that they have a romantic relationship with, and is usually always on the defense. They truly believe that nobody should be, or can be trusted, because everybody in their past have all done them wrong. This has lead them to believe that everybody that they encounter are the same types of "messed-up people" that they have encountered in their past. If any of these types of behaviors sound familiar to you, then you may be, or may know of a person that is "Bitterly-Insecure".

Many years of abuse, neglect, betrayal, insults, and all-around poor treatment, causes an insecure person to always be on the defense or want to "one-up" a person so that they can feel that they have some kind of advantage. No longer do they want to be on the receiving end of being or feeling hurt, so they instead try to do the hurting of others before they can hurt them.

For instance, have you ever heard of a person that was so insecure of themselves and their relationship, that they decided to do something silly like cheat on their partner *before* their partner got the chance to cheat on them? Or have you ever heard of a person that puts someone down and makes them feel bad about themselves so that somebody else can feel the same level of insecurity that they feel? Or maybe a person that has a bunch of other people lined up for them to get into relationships with just in case their partner doesn't feel as strongly about the relationship as they do, and decides to break up with them? Well if you have heard of such scenarios, then you know of a person that is Bitterly-Insecure. Bitterly-Insecure people are always trying to be one step ahead, just incase something unfortunate happens to them, and ends up making them feel even more insecure about themselves than they already do.

Bitterly-Insecure is only one of the many types of people that us insecure individuals can become after spending a long period of time being manipulated, hurt, and/or taken advantage of. Some of those things that we can also become are terms that I like to refer to as *"Sexually-Insecure", "Clingy-Insecure"*, and *"Passively-Insecure"*. Each type or category has its own unique yet very similar qualities. Allow me to explain and give my definitions of each term.

Sexually-Insecure people are those of us that begin to use our bodies, looks, and sex as a coping mechanism and a way to feel good about ourselves. Internally, we have low self-esteem and don't think highly of who we are, so we try to mask these inner thoughts and feelings with vanity and sexual pleasure. We may find ourselves in many flings that never result into meaningful relationships, and/or have a hard time connecting to people on a more personal and deeper level. Sexually-Insecure people prefer to live life as freely as possible because they fear becoming too attached and possibly getting hurt.

Most people that are Sexually-Insecure will appear to be very confident on the outside. They may be well put together, charismatic, and very outgoing people. They try to shield their insecurity by using the blanket of being "sexually free", "body-positive", and "social-butterflies". They desperately want to feel love on a deeper and more meaningful level, but choose to settle for surface-level connections instead.

These types of individuals look for love, acceptance, and validation, based upon how many people are sexually attracted to them. They view attention and infatuation as "love", and when they don't receive it, they feel unwanted and unsure of themselves. Sexually-Insecure individuals always need to feel that they are the center of attention because when they are not, their insecurities of not feeling good enough, attractive enough, and or loved enough, begin to rise to the surface causing them to act out. They then may begin to try to draw attention to themselves by being overly sexual, overly flirtatious, and wild. There are many more attributes to people that are Sexually-Insecure and those are just to name a few.

You may be someone that is Sexually-Insecure or you may know of someone that is, and want desperately not to be this person that is constantly looking for love and acceptance through the physical. You probably don't even understand how or why you became this Sexually-Insecure person to begin with. Maybe it was due to not being properly loved. Maybe it was due to being constantly rejected or not feeling attractive. Maybe it was from being sexually abused or emotionally abused. Whatever the case is, it is important for those of us that are Sexually-Insecure to know and understand that we are more than our bodies. We have so much more to offer the world than orgasmic sex, sex-appeal, and lust. We deserve more than surface-level love and need to surround ourselves with people that want to know us for who we truly are as human-beings and not just for what we have to offer sexually or physically.

Its important for those of us that are Sexually-Insecure to refrain from sexual interaction for a while so that we can get to the root causes as to why we feel the need to have relations that are only on that level. We need to take some time to figure out who we are outside of just our looks, and sexuality. Cut people off that seem to only want to be involved with you physically and surround yourself with people that you feel are genuinely into you as a person.

If everyone around you seems to only want you in their presence for surface-level interactions, then it is best for you to simply be alone.

While you are alone, do a lot of self-reflecting or "soul-searching", so that you can figure things out on your own and perhaps attract new people into your life to associate with. People that genuinely love and care about you want to be in your life outside of just sex, partying, and other surface-level reasons. Do your best to get to the root causes as to why you are choosing to express yourself in this way, and find a healthier and more honest approach of dealing with, and confronting your insecurities, head-on

There are also some of us that are struggling with our insecurities so much so, that we become the type of people that are what I like to refer to as *"Clingy-Insecure"* individuals. *Clingy-Insecure* people are those of us that are so fearful of being abandoned, left behind, and forgotten, that we become obsessively attached to a person, and feel anxious, sad, and unable to function without them. Oftentimes, a Clingy-Insecure person is a serial-dater and hops from one relationship to the next because they cant stand the thought of being alone. Being alone makes a Clingy-Insecure person feel as though they are not worthy enough to be with someone and forces them to have to deal with their insecurities. They would much rather like to be distracted by the company of someone that they are romantically involved with.

Clingy-Insecure people are usually very smothering in relationships. They must know the whereabouts, the small details, and every move of their significant other to make sure that they are not straying away from them. At any given moment, a Clingy-Insecure person can blow up and cause a scene if they begin to feel that their partner is distancing themselves, or wants to spend time away from them. This triggers something internally with the Clingy-Insecure person and makes them once again feel as though they are not good enough to keep the interest or attention of their significant other.

In most instances, Clingy-Insecure people end up pushing their partners away by being way too demanding of their time and attention. This causes their partner to feel as though they can not live their lives as they see fit, which leads them to want to leave the relationship altogether. Clingy-Insecure individuals do not understand that their extreme attachment to their significant other is not healthy, which leads them to continue on with their clinginess. They do not understand that it is perfectly fine for them to allow their partner space and time without them.

It is important for those of us that are Clingy-Insecure individuals to know and understand that we are good enough with or without someone. Relationships don't validate us or make us any better than we already are. We must begin to feel whole alone, and stop looking for other things and people outside of ourselves to bring us peace and happiness.

This leads me to the *"Passively-Insecure"* individuals. *Passively-Insecure* people are those of us that have become so accustomed to being mistreated by people, that we now have become numb to it. They are very dismissive, nonchalant, and don't seem to care about much at all concerning relationships with people, because they feel as though the relationship will be doomed to fail anyway.

Passively-Insecure people have a hard time really trying to connect with others. They prefer to be isolated and alone, and have little to no interaction. A Passively-Insecure person feels that if they limit their company or interactions with other people, then they lower the chances of them becoming too involved or invested into a person or a situation, and getting hurt.

Someone that is Passively-Insecure may enter into a relationship but will still have their guards up so that they do not become too emotionally attached. They prefer to always establish barriers regardless of how involved they are with a person, just so that no one can become too close. Even if a Passively-Insecure person truly feels strongly about someone, they will not show this, and do their best to remain at a nice distance. This may cause their partner to feel as though they are not truly interested in the relationship, and drift away.

Once a relationship is over, Passively-Insecure people will not display any sort of emotional distress over the situation. Deep down inside, they already expected for the relationship not to last very long or go very far, so they are already mentally prepared for the break-up. Relationships are not much of a priority for a Passively-Insecure person; so when a break-up does occur, they are perfectly fine with going without another relationship for quite some time.

In many instances, Passively-Insecure people will come off to be very closed-off, uninviting, and secluded. To the average person, they seem to be introverts, but they are really just very insecure people that are trying to steer clear of any kind of social interaction, in hopes of not being rejected. Passively-Insecure individuals secretly care very much about connecting with others and maintaining relationships, but have to uphold the persona of not caring as a coping mechanism. They think that as long as they pretend not to really care, they will avoid not really being hurt.

Passively insecure people need to know and understand that simply pretending not to care about the opinions of others, relationships, being accepted, and loved, is doing more damage than good. When you put guards up and try to avoid being too open with people, you are only suppressing the issue. This will cause your emotions to build up and possibly explode once a situation presents itself that you are not too fond of. You need to know that it is okay to allow yourself to be vulnerable. You are not preventing anything from getting to you by acting as if its not. Allow yourself to feel. Allow yourself to open up and be inviting of people that are showing you that they genuinely care about you and your well-being.

There are many other things that us insecure people can become if we do not take time out to work on ourselves and come out of our insecurities. We can even be a mixture of all of the things mentioned above. This is why it is very important for us to recognize that we have a problem with being insecure, so that we may take the proper precautions. Going through life inflicting harm on ourselves, and those around us, does nothing but continues on the cycle of hurt, pain, and misery. It is time for us to stop being the "hurt people that are hurting people"; and most of all it is time for us to stop being the hurt people that are hurting OURSELVES.

CHAPTER 5: The Realization Of What We've Become

We have now reached the point where we have realized that there is a problem that we need to change and fix from within. We have recognized patterns with the relationships we continue to get ourselves involved in, and also the kind of individuals that we are. It has come to our attention that the kinds of people that we surround ourselves with as well as the things that we like to indulge in, are unhealthy. Now it is time that we become honest with ourselves and do some real self-reflecting and self-work.

Its not easy coming to the conclusion that you are a major part of the reason as to why you find yourself in so many toxic situations. It is much easier for us to blame everything outside of self, than to take accountability for the poor choices we choose to make. This is one of the main reasons as to why it may take so long for many of us that are struggling with insecurities to actually take a step back and look in the mirror. We are afraid that the mirror will show us too many of the flaws and lies that we have been projecting onto other people to make us feel not as responsible.

I too was once that person that had a very difficult time accepting fault for all the terrible things, people, and situations that I was getting myself involved with. I didn't understand that these negative things and people always found their way back to me because there was something going on internally with me that was inviting these things and people into my life. No one can come into your life and disrupt it or cause you harm unless you give it permission to, and that's the part we are all missing. Once I realized that I was the person that was responsible for my own happiness, peace, and well-being, it was time for me to make some changes.

Nobody but you can bring you happiness and peace. Nobody but you can make you feel confident and secure within yourself. There's no amount of money, nice clothes, cars, houses, make-up, or jewelry that can make you feel that you are worthy. Feeling worthy starts with you *knowing* that you are good enough *without* all of those things. It may take some time to finally get to that point, but you will get there with the right mindset and self-discipline.

I had to do some real work on myself. It started with first knowing that I was the problem. Drama was following me because I WAS DRAMA. Pain was following me because I WAS PAIN. Broken people were coming into my life because I WAS BROKEN. Once I realized this, I had to heal myself from the inside out. My mindset of being the victim had to be stripped from me. My mindset of not being in control of my life and what happens in my life, had to be erased. I had to take responsibility and accountability, and it was the hardest thing that I ever had to do.

Taking accountability and responsibility pulled the wool from my eyes and forced me to look at myself through a more critical lens. I couldn't make myself out to be this angel that everybody was mistreating and hurting for no particular reason. It showed me my faults and flaws, and it was uncomfortable. I was starting to see myself as a bad person, and that made me feel even more insecure about myself.

When you are having an awakening about yourself and your role in your bad circumstances, all sorts of emotions and thoughts will come pouring into you. You will feel a heaviness to you because you now have to be the person that says "I Should Have Done Better For Myself". All of those times you spent pointing the finger at "fill in the blank", you now have to hold yourself accountable for allowing "fill in the blank" to come into your life and continue to cause you pain and suffering in the first place. It's a hard pill to swallow knowing that you are the one to blame for most of your failures, and that's why we choose to just run away from getting to the root causes of our problems. Now, there are some cases where what happened to you was not your fault and you had absolutely no control over it. However, what you choose to do after the fact, *is*. Fortunately for you, you are choosing to stop running and face your issues so that you can conquer them, and stop this insanity.

You should be proud of yourself. Something has finally hit you and made you wake up from your slumber. You have noticed that there is a common denominator in all of the equations, and that common denominator is *YOU*. You have looked at every situation for what it *really* is, and not for what you want to make it up to be in your mind. You now see the harsh realities of situations and people, and are no longer living in the fantasy-world. Even if it means you looking like the "bad-guy", you are now ready and willing to deal with people and things in a truthful and honest way.

As I stated before, it was hard for me to finally get to this level in my life where I was finally ready to no longer be the victim. Being the victim makes us feel as though we are innocent and blame-free. It helps us to be able to live with ourselves, and continue on living our lives as guilt-free as we possibly can. It helps us to lie to ourselves so that the next time will be even easier for us to feel as though we are these perfect little angels that do no harm; and everybody else are the evil ones. But being the victim also keeps us in the dark and keeps us from ever growing and elevating.

When I decided to stop being the victim, it stripped away from me my crutch. I subconsciously liked being able to blame my problems on other things and people outside of myself, because it made me feel as though I was doing nothing wrong, and didn't have to do any work on myself. Having that kind of mentality was hurting me more than it was helping me. It was allowing me to be complacent in my misery and continue on with the same kind of treatment and behavior that was making me unhappy in the first place.

You have to make the conscious decision to rid yourself of being the person that is always the victim, so that you can start to see your place in all of the chaos and madness. The only way that you can fix the problem is to know why the problem exists to begin with. And most times, the problems are in our lives because we have somehow allowed them to be. I was *allowing* things and people to be in my life that I knew without a shadow of a doubt did not belong. I was making excuses for people as well as for myself as to why things were the way that they were. This was doing nothing but allowing things to remain as they were; dysfunctional.

Now that you have made the conscious decision to make the proper changes to live your best life and be the best version of yourself, you have to *fully commit* to those changes. You cannot allow yourself to be the same person as you were before. You can't allow yourself to be okay with mistreatment and unhappiness. You have to always choose peace and rid yourself of anybody and anything that may disrupt your peace. Even if you feel as though you love that person or care for them deeply, a person that is causing you heartache and suffering, must GO.

Getting rid of people that are causing you harm or contributing to your peace of mind being disrupted, can be a difficult task, ironically. Coming to the conclusion that you have to eliminate your interactions or limit your interactions with people that you have feelings for, can make you feel uneasy and heartless. But you have to put your feelings to the side and think logically. You must do what you know is best for YOU first, and that means being ok with letting go of unhealthy things and people. Initially it will be difficult for you to do, but you will eventually grow to understand that it is ok for you to be selfish in this instance. Your happiness is more important than anything, and it is time for you to stop doing the same things over and over again expecting for things and people to change. If the results are always the same, then it is time *for you to do something different.*

The things that I had to do differently were change my victim mindset, change my circle of friends (family included), engage in healthy activities like reading helpful books, eating better, and exercising, practicing positive affirmations, and facing the demons from my past. I knew that I could not go into a new and improved better version of myself by being the same person that I was. After all, being the type of person that I was, was the exact reason why I was in this type of predicament to begin with. I had to shed myself of who I was so that I could go into my evolution as wholesome as I could. I didn't need bad thoughts, bad energy, and bad habits hindering me.

This is what we all must do once we come to the realization that we are not the people that we want to be. We must cleanse ourselves; mind, body, and soul, so that we can go into our evolutionary stage as pure as possible. We do not need things that we know will trigger us or bring us back to our low states of thought and energy around us. It takes much work and discipline, but it MUST BE DONE.

Chapter 6: Overcoming Our Insecurities

We've now reached the part of the story where its time to not only *recognize* our faults and issues, but to actually *do something about them.* It's not enough to just *know* that there is an issue if you're not going to come up with and *act upon a solution.* There are many of us that know we have a problem dealing with our insecurities, but have no clue where to start as far as overcoming it. This chapter will help to shed some light on some of the things that you can do to begin your journey to overcoming your insecurities.

Well, the good news is, you have already taken the first step to overcoming your issue of being and feeling insecure. The fact that you were honest enough to pick up this book and read it so that you can gain a clearer understanding of what's going on with you as far as the issue of insecurity is concerned, shows that you are well on your way to overcoming it. There are so many people that simply dwell in their misery and do absolutely nothing but complain. You, however, have done enough complaining and decided to take accountability and action; and you should be proud of yourself for that.

It shows a great level of maturity and growth for someone to admit that they have a problem. Many of us have way too much pride to be able to do any kind of self-work, even if we know that it needs to be done. Part of the first step to overcoming your insecurity issue is recognizing that you have a problem, and taking steps, big or small, to annihilate them. Since you have already completed the first step, you can now move on to the second step of overcoming your insecurity issue; which is to **_"Forgive the Past"_**.

As mentioned in the previous chapters, many of our insecurities stem from our childhood or things that happened to us in the past that we have a difficult time letting go of. It is important for those of us that are harboring and holding on to those past traumas, to forgive those people that are responsible, so that we can learn to heal properly and move forward with our lives. We can not evolve into the best versions of ourselves, if we are holding on to the past versions of ourselves, and what happened to us.

We must learn to forgive and let go of that pain and hurt so that we can transmute it into strength, power, peace, and love. This will not be easy due to the fact that many of us have very deep scars from our past that have not been treated for a very long time. Nonetheless, it's crucial for us to face those demons of our past and kill them so that we are not taking those same demons into the next chapter of our life. The goal is to let go of those past traumas so that it does not begin to damage anything that is good for us, in the future. Again, this wont be easy and it won't happen overnight. Forgiving a situation and/or an individual that may have hurt you and caused you a great deal of pain and suffering over the course of many years, can make you feel as though you are somehow giving that person a pass. But you are not. You are acknowledging the fact that this person or situation hurt you, and you are deciding to take back your power in a healthy way by deciding to accept that it happened, and moving forward. You no longer will give this person or situation any room to steal and take your joy and peace. From now on, you will be the person that is taking control of your life and your peace of mind.

In order to forgive, you have to acknowledge that this person or situation hurt you. You cannot continue acting as if this situation never occurred, or harboring those ill thoughts and feeling hoping that it will one day go away on its own. It won't. You have to express your pain whether it is directly to that person that hurt you, or expressing it through writing, or to a person that you trust. Once you release that pain, you will now be able to do the necessary and healthy things that you see fit to help you to heal those wounds. But you will not be able to do that until you face those past traumas, and start releasing those emotions, so that you can finally let go.

The next step in overcoming your insecurity is to **_"Accept ALL of You"._** Just the same as you have now accepted the fact that you are suffering from being insecure, and accepting the fact that things happened to you in the past that you will now forgive and move on from; you now have to learn to fully love, appreciate, and accept YOURSELF. You must realize that you are not perfect and will never be; just the same as the rest of us. However, that doesn't give you the right to degrade yourself and bring yourself down.

As mentioned before, there are many of us that are so accustomed to being mistreated, talked down to, and abused, that we have now learned to do the same exact things to ourselves. And just the same as over the years you have learned to be cruel to yourself, you now have to take some time to learn to be nice to yourself and show some love and compassion. You must know and understand that it took a while for you to reach this state of insecurity that you are in, and it might take just as long for you to unlearn this poor behavior and treatment of yourself. Give yourself some time to learn and grow, and try your best not to be so hard on yourself.

Take a self-assessment. Analyze the parts of yourself, both mentally and physically that you do not like. Whether it's the way your body looks, the way your smile is, or your pitiful outlook on life, learn to send and give those imperfect parts of yourself, LOVE. You not only need it, but you DESERVE IT.

Its okay to not feel 100% satisfied with yourself. That's part of being human. But give yourself credit. LOTS of credit. Know and understand that your mind and body might not be exactly where you want them to be today at this very moment; but with the right patience, love, and understanding, you will get there. Also, know and understand that there may be parts of you that you probably wont be able to change, and learn to embrace them anyway. Self-Love is genuinely the best love. Since you are the person that will have to live with yourself day in and day out for the rest of your life, you might as well get used to loving yourself and doing all that you can to ensure your own peace and happiness. Nobody outside of yourself can bring you any peace, happiness, or validation. Thus, get used to accepting yourself, loving yourself, and embracing yourself.

You NEED you.

The next step to overcoming your insecurity issues is to **"Stay Away From Negative Thoughts".** As you already know, this is something that will take much practice and time to master; especially as a person that spent so much time being hard on themselves. But just because this may be something that may take lots of practice, time, and dedication to break the habit of, doesn't mean that it can't be done.

Like I stated before, I was the person that was overly critical of myself and believed all of the negative things people were saying about me (ugly, lame, geeky, dirty, etc) It took much time to stop seeing myself in that negative light and to start praising myself. I decided that the only way I could stop having negative thoughts and feelings about myself, was to stop associating with negative people. Most times we have negative thoughts because we are surrounding ourselves with negative people that are bringing us down. And the scariest part about this, is most times we don't even know we are associating with such gloomy, negative, pessimistic individuals. This is why it is important to do an assessment on the people that you allow into your company. As I have stated before, you will sometimes have to limit your time with people, or cut people off completely, if they display signs of being those types of gloomy, negative, pessimistic individuals. This will be difficult to do, but it is essential to your self-growth and development.

Aside from doing your absolute best to stay away from negative people to make sure your mind is clear and positive, you can also write down some positive affirmations for yourself to repeat and read aloud to yourself daily. Simply take out a piece of paper and a pen and write down as many positive things about yourself so that it serves as a constant reminder of how exceptional you are. One of the affirmations I wrote down for myself a few years ago when I was feeling low was "I'm Happy. I'm Healthy. I'm Progressing. I'm Beautiful. I am at Peace." I said this aloud to myself daily and slowly but surely I would start to feel that I was all of those positive things. At first it may feel silly or awkward saying those things aloud to yourself, but after a while you will catch on. Once you get used to reading and saying those positive words about yourself daily, take it a step further and look yourself in the eyes with a smile in the mirror and do the same thing. It may be weird or seem funny initially, but positive affirmations can definitely help in regards to changing your negative thoughts into positive thoughts.

Changing your mindset is the most important step of them all since what we think is what we feel, and what we feel we will become. If you think lowly of yourself, you will feel low, which will ultimately result into you being low. You cannot allow yourself to steal your own happiness and joy by constantly being a victim and a slave to your poor thoughts. Snap out of beating yourself up and become your own biggest fan, cheerleader, and supporter. Get in the habit of complimenting yourself, praising yourself, and giving yourself credit where and when its due. Don't be overly critical and judgmental. When you make a mistake or don't like something about yourself at a particular time, say motivational things to yourself so that you will do better next time. There is no need to kick yourself while you're down.

When you are trying to get into the habit of eliminating your negative thoughts, you may also find yourself comparing yourself to other people and situations. You need to get into the habit of reversing those envious feelings and turning them into motivation and positivity. For example if Carlos or Amanda next door has a nice car or is attractive etc, don't compare your car or looks to theirs. Instead, say Carlos/Amanda has a nice car and I admire that. I will work hard so that I too can get a car that I would like. Or Carlos/Amanda is very attractive, but I am also attractive in my own right and will do what I can to embrace my own great qualities. Everything is about perspective; and when your perspective is positive, your thoughts will be positive too.

The next step to overcoming your insecurities is to **_"Invest Into Your Passions"_**. Insecurities have a way of trying to hinder you from what's important to you in life. We can spend so much time being afraid, uncertain, unsure, and doubtful, that we begin to place our hopes, dreams, and aspirations on the back-burner. We have to break out of that and become more confident in ourselves so that we may attain all of the great things that we want, need, and deserve out of life. Pursuing your passions is a great instrument that you can use to help you overcome your insecurities.

Investing more of your time, energy, and creativity into one or more of your passions, can allow you to gain the confidence that you need by giving you more meaning and purpose to your life. When you have something to work on or look forward to, it helps you to become more outgoing and ambitious. This in and of itself can cause a domino-effect, causing you to become even more energetic about life, making you want to branch out and do more. Investing into your passions will help you to build up your strengths, skills, and abilities, which will ultimately lead you to build up your self-esteem and confidence.

Simply find something that interests you, and focus on building upon it. Many of us don't take the time out to explore our passions which results into us feeling like we don't have a place in this world, and that we are not important. Once you find something that you feel will bring you some sort of peace, purpose, and excitement out of life, you will be so focused on that said thing, that you will slowly but surely start to feel less and less meaningless and insignificant. If we all could simply learn to follow and work towards our dreams and goals, we would be so motivated upon that passion that we would stop dwelling and focusing on our faults and insecurities.

The last step toward overcoming your insecurities is to **_"Repeat Each Step Daily"._** Everything is all about repetition. You can not break a bad habit without constantly doing whatever it takes to avoid doing those bad habits, everyday. Just like it took lots of repetition for you to fall victim to being insecure, it will take just as much repetition of those POSITIVE things to bring you out of being insecure.

Its okay if some days are harder than the others. However, you must stick to the program. After reading this book, you should have done a lot of self-reflecting and seeing why you have become insecure, and what you have become from being insecure. And since you now have some sort of general idea of the "why's" and "how's" you should be able to know exactly what it is going to take to bring you out of this miserable insecure state that you are currently in. It will take much effort, dedication, and sheer will to bring you out on the other side, but you must have enough faith in yourself to do it.

We all suffer from our own demons; even the people that you will least expect. However, it's the work, time, effort, and energy you put into changing your perspective from negative to positive, and holding yourself accountable for becoming a better person. There is nothing or no one in this world that is better than you, stronger than you, or more capable than you. So get out of the mindset of things being "too complicated" or impossible for you to do. You can overcome your battles just as the next person and should not feel that you are defeated.

Get out of the habit of thinking that you are weak. Get out of the habit of feeling like you are not good enough. Get out of the habit of being okay with the bare minimum. Removing that poor mindset will cause you to push yourself to great heights, and get what you deserve out of yourself and out of life. You are a phenomenal human being, and people should treat you as such. If people can not give you the quality treatment that you deserve, they must be checked and/or eliminated.

You are on a constant journey to greatness and elevation. You cannot afford to give up on yourself as many people in your past have done. This road and journey wont be an easy one, but it is a necessary one that you must travel everyday until you feel that you have reached a level of peace, self-love, and confidence. By making sure that you repeat each step daily, you are sure to rewire and reprogram yourself to do just that.

Be sure to remind yourself that you are not your past mistakes. What you choose to accept right here and right now is what defines you and makes you. Along this path to self-love there will be plenty of bumps in the road. There will be days that you may feel as though you can't push forward and make it through. There may be days where you feel as though you aren't good enough and will never be good enough for anybody or yourself. You must know and understand that you are human and its perfectly fine to have those days. BUT GET BACK UP.

Though its fine for you to have bad days where you don't feel or think your best, it is NOT okay to stay in that frame of mind. When you feel low, get out that piece of paper with those positive affirmations and read them. When you feel bad, look at yourself in the mirror and tell yourself how amazing you are. When you feel yourself becoming jealous, or comparing yourself to the next person, remind yourself that you are just as special as anybody else. You are DONE with that pitiful behavior and that chapter of your life is CLOSED.

It is a new and improved YOU. Those poor qualities and characteristics are no longer welcome into your life. You will now vibrate on a higher and more positive frequency which will attract more positive things and situations to you. You will now find yourself always being met with good and quality news because that's the law of attraction. What you focus on grows; and in this case you are focused on positivity and elevation. Thus, you will be met with positivity and elevation.

You will no longer allow poor-minded or poor-spirited people into your company because you will feel their poor energy and repel it away from you. Gone are the days when you allowed people to come into your life to use you and take advantage of you. Now, only people that want to lift you up and bring you positivity are welcome. Gone are the days when you want to hurt people because you are hurting. You will now only want to lift people up and give them love because you now have uplifted yourself and gave yourself the love that you were so desperately craving. You now have begun to stop seeking things and people outside of yourself to make you happy and bring you peace, because you understand that only you can give YOURSELF those things.

Insecurity is no longer something that you will be suffering from. You have made the commitment to do whatever it is that needs to be done for you to prosper in this world. Your guards are no longer hindering you from developing deep and meaningful relationships, and your mind is no longer that of a victim. There is nothing that you can not accomplish and overcome because you now know and understand that you are powerful and victorious.

Your past is your past, and you are now focused on your future. You know that your future will be bright because you know that you are in charge of your future, the company that you keep, and the thoughts that enter your mind. Nobody will ever again be able to manipulate you, destroy your positive perception of yourself, or control you because you will never give anybody that kind of power over you again. You are the captain of your fate and the master of your soul.

CLOSING

I hope that this book was very beneficial for those of you that took the time out to read it. I hope that I was able to give you a little bit of clarity and direction towards overcoming your internal battle with insecurity and giving you hope for the future. You are only as great as you think that you are, and most of the battle is mental. Once you are able to know and understand that your mind is powerful, you will begin to choose more wisely about the things that you put into your mind.

Nobody is perfect and you should not hold yourself to impossible standards. Everything takes time and you should take time with yourself. Do not rush your process. Move along at your own speed and at your own pace. Do not become angry, discouraged, or disappointed if you happen to fall back into the same types of behaviors that you are trying to escape. Just acknowledge that you had a slip up, and then go back to the necessary courses of action or steps to reverse that negative behavior.

Life is all about growth and elevation, and sometimes during our journey of growth and elevation we may tend to have unfortunate things happen to us. However, its important for us to realize that its not about WHAT happens to us, but HOW WE CHOOSE TO RESPOND. Always choose the higher road and look for the good in the bad. There is always something of great value or a great lesson that can be gained from every situation. Thus, do not allow those bad things, people, or situations to define you. YOU DEFINE YOU.

And always remember…

YOU ARE WORTHY.

www.ingramcontent.com/pod-product-compliance
Lightning Source LLC
Chambersburg PA
CBHW031159160426
43193CB00008B/440